Blossom English

TOEM Books

www.to-em.com

John Stephen Knodell

ISBN – 978-4-908152-18-4

Toem Books
〒064-0822 北海道札幌市Chuo Ward, 北2条西26丁目2-18 4F-A
Sapporo, Japan

Dedicated to

Hard Word

How to Use the Book

The Blossom English series is a content-based textbook that uses authentic readings with grammar, writing, and speaking exercises. While the textbook is rich with grammar exercises, exercises can be used to A) create conversations from the grammar exercises B) test students on the problematic grammar points throughout the book, and C) connect the reading book with sections of the textbook, for example, the making perfect sentences and grammar focus sections.

For classes studying English approximately 3-4 hours a week, try to finish one reading section, one grammar focus/preposition/article exercise, and one writing assignment. Each week, test students on one of the grammar exercises, have a review test of the vocabulary, and always use the textbook as an opportunity to speak with students. In order to prepare for writing essays, debate the topic before giving the assignment for homework.

About the Author

John Stephen Knodell has an M.Ed. in TESOL, and has been an English language teacher for over 20 years. He has taught students from 2 years old to students over 80, from private classes to classes of over 100 students. He currently teaches at a university in Japan and runs Toem Languages.

Table of Contents

THE BOY WHO TALKED WITH ANIMALS

PART 1

VOCABULARY TO LEARN

with a thud, met his end, precisely, a terrific fuss, swaying, keels right over, stalking, flicked,

motionless, prancing, queer, courtship ritual, a commotion, trooping down, bilious, detour,

domed, loincloth, flippers, spectacle, spectacles, paunchy, bid you higher

QUESTIONS

1. Who is the narrator in this story and describe him?

2. What was dangerous about coconuts?

3. What great commotion happened on the man's second day?

4. How large was the turtle?

5. How were the men acting masculine?

6. Describe the man who wanted to buy the turtle.

7. Why does the hotel not talk about the coconut accident?

8. What is the atmosphere in this story so far?

VOCABULARY TO LEARN

consumption, dignified, clobbered, a touch, splendid scheme, wobbled, patronizing voice, heave, shrill, wriggling, restrain, a bit off balance, honourable, addressing the crowd, shuffling their feet, uneasiness, restraining, dodged, swerved, lunge, stricken, agonized wail

QUESTIONS

1. Why was the narrator upset at the people on the beach?

2. What would happen if the men tipped the turtle over?

3. What made the men stop pulling the turtle?

4. How did the boy's parents feel about the boy's complaints?

5. Why did the people on the beach feel shame?

6. Why wouldn't the boy listen to his mother telling him not to go to the turtle?

7. How many men did it take to pull the turtle?

8. Why is the turtle's age important to the narrator?

VOCABULARY TO LEARN

a pace, lethal, slaughtered, hysterical, communicates, gruesome, a fraction of, a bribe, fiercest,

aghast, guarantee, as long as, immensely, wedged, intimate, waddling, sedately, the horizon,

subdued, bantering, not the end of the affair

QUESTIONS

1. What deal did the father make with the manager?

2. Describe the manager.

3. Why was the manager of the hotel worried (not about the boy)?

4. How long couldn't the fishermen catch the turtle?

5. What is the plot in this story so far?

6. What is a theme in this story concerning people?

7. How did the turtle react after being turned over?

8. Describe the relationship between the boy and the turtle.

VOCABULARY TO LEARN

big fuss, faintly glazed, pointless, natives, paddling, skimmed, his chest heaving, nodding

vigorously, creeping, urging, beached, lent a hand, trousers, no trace of, uninhabited,

significant, approaching yacht

QUESTIONS

1. If you saw a turtle trapped by men, what would you do?

2. How does the setting in the beginning reflect the action in the story?

3. Why weren't the policemen surprised about the two fishermen?

4. Summarize what they saw in one sentence.

5. Why would the boy choose to live with a turtle?

6. How would the boy's parents feel about the ending of the story?

7. What is the style of writing in this story?

8. Who is your favourite character? Why?

THE SWAN

VOCABULARY TO LEARN

rifle, slouching, nab, brown ale, pound note, pinchin', shootin' yer month off, physical

violence, everyday occurrence, insulting, shrill, sanctuary, daft, binocular, twerp, detested,

freckled, spectacles, pupil, a slug, guts, confess, pointless

QUESTIONS

1.   What did Ernie's father want him to do with the rifle?

2.   How does Ernie's father treat him?

3.   Describe Ernie.

4.   What did Ernie do at soccer games?

5.   Why did the boys go to the countryside?

6.   Why didn't Ernie and Raymond like Peter Watson?

7. How do the boys know each other?

_____

8. Why wasn't Peter afraid?

_____

9. What did Ernie and Raymond think Peter was doing?

_____

10. Why couldn't Peter run away?

_____

VOCABULARY TO LEARN

timid, suspiciously, cheeky, stuck-up, intently, this winded him, trussed up, wriggle,

threading, virtually, immobile, clearance, scrape 'im, swollen, gravel, indentation, kept an eye

open, deafening, limp, stiff, tense, vibrating, scarcely audible, a speck, shattering

QUESTIONS

1. Why was Peter watching birds?

_____

2. What would happen if Peter didn't keep his hands up?

_____

3. How did Ernie and Raymond prevent Peter from moving?

4. Where did Ernie and Raymond bring Peter, and why?

5. Why might the train hit Peter, but not other people?

6. How often did the trains pass?

7. How did Peter save himself from being hit by the train (give 2 answers)?

8. How did Peter not think about the coming danger?

9. How did Peter know the train was coming?

10. Why didn't Ernie and Raymond let Peter go?

 P.86-93

VOCABULARY TO LEARN

provoking, no doubt whatsoever, boasting, wrecked, interiors, pedestrians, be passive,

aggravate, willow trees, flush, strictly forbidden, fetch, binding, disturbed, serenely, sneering,

waded out, tenderly, outburst, malicious manner, demented, the kisser, resistance

QUESTIONS

1. What did hooligans do?

2. What was Peter's plan to be free?

3. What mistake did Peter make?

4. Why weren't people allowed to shoot birds at the lake?

5. What promise did Ernie make Peter?

6. Which bird was the most protected bird in England?

7. Why did Peter lie about the swan's eggs?

8. What did Ernie plan to do with the swan?

9. Why was Ernie able to cut birds so well?

10. If you were Peter, what would you do?

VOCABULARY TO LEARN

securely, surveying, grotesquely, halted, as though, appealed to him, tormentors, dreaded,

sparse, slender, knocked off, the thigh, devastating, driven beyond the point of endurance,

crumple, unconquerable, beckoning

QUESTIONS

1. How did Ernie bring the swan back to life?

2. What did Ernie want Peter to do?

3. Why was Peter happy to climb the tree?

4. What happened when Peter didn't jump off the branch?

5. Did Peter feel pain when Ernie shot him? Explain.

6. What happened to Peter when he got shot?

7. How was Peter a special person when faced with problems?

8. What do you think the light was at the end of the story?

_____

9. Where did Peter fly?

_____

10. How do you feel about this story?

_____

THE WONDERFUL STORY OF
HENRY SUGAR

VOCABULARY TO LEARN

tailor, trimmed, a manicure, capped, tinge, mole, a cottage, inherited, incur, insatiable

longing, roulette, blackjack, high stakes, wagered, idle, pelting, croquet, glumly, resentful,

ambled aimlessly, rubbish, a motto

QUESTIONS

1. How did Henry get his money?

2. What did his motto mean?

3. What do all wealthy people have in common?

4. How did he make money from his dog?

5. Why was Henry upset at Sir William Wyndham's home?

6. What kind of character was Henry, and how do you know this?

7. How did Henry feel about classic novels?

8. What is one possible plot in this story?

VOCABULARY TO LEARN

well-earned, firmly, lids, clenched, a peg, genuine, a private matter, billed on the program,

expert fashion, applied, a hard film, a basin, plastered, proceeded, giddy, swathed, strolling

casually, rigid, surged, a placard

QUESTIONS

1. When were people allowed into the doctor's room?

2. How did the doctors test the blind man?

3. What didn't the blind man tell the doctors?

4. Why did the blind man visit the hospital?

5. Why was it important that the blind man see doctors?

6. How could people remove colodion?

7. What did the doctors have to make sure of when bandaging the blind man?

8. What are 3 acts that surprised the doctors?

CHAPTER 3 P.111-115

VOCABULARY TO LEARN

off duty, my flat, furnace, seeping out, milling around, conjurors, thoroughly, utensils, ,

turbans, keep his balance, a revolver, accuracy, within a hairsbreath, flabbergasted, , solemnly,

consent, no objection, emerged

QUESTIONS

1. How hot was it in Bombay in summer?

2. How long was the show?

3. Which act by Khan impressed Dr. Cartwright the most?

4. What made the audience scream with excitement?

5. What favour did the doctor ask of Khan?

6. Why was it good that a doctor wrote Khan's life story?

7. Why did Dr. Cartwright want to write Khan's story?

8. What made Cartwright flabbergasted?

CHAPTER 4 P.115-124

VOCABULARY TO LEARN

rupees, a bombshell, disciple, fanatically, despise, sum, levitation, suspended, the banks,

absolute seclusion, by nature, slight of hand, dense, dismount, rustling, meditates, a raffle,

brass, incense, serenity, deception, he stirs, wonderstruck

QUESTIONS

1. How does Dahl make the reader feel this is a true story?

2. What made Khan run away from home?

3. What made Khan very disappointed?

4. What kind of people are yogis?

5. What couldn't yogis do, and what would happen if they did?

6. What was special about Banerjee?

7. How did Khan find Banerjee?

8. What was Khan unsure of while watching Banerjee?

<table>
<tr><td>CHAPTER 5</td><td>P.124-129</td></tr>
</table>

VOCABULARY TO LEARN

consents, critical part, eager pupil, conscious mind, scattered, humble, a rajah, making

progress, earn a living, a trench, stoking, obliged, singed, the soles, the hem, a trance

QUESTIONS

1. Why did Khan go to Hardawar?

2. What was the critical part of the instruction?

3. What is the problem with the conscious mind?

4. What kind of people were one in a million?

5. How did Khan practice his concentration?

6. What did he lose because of his practicing?

7. How did Khan know he was on his way to becoming a yogi?

<table>
<tr><td>CHAPTER 6</td><td>P129-133</td></tr>
</table>

VOCABULARY TO LEARN

omit, mauve, level with, queer, the outline, conveying, striving, the pack, blindfold, bare, out

of sight, at random, stationed myself, quiver, antennae, perceptive

QUESTIONS

1. What does Khan dedicate his life to after walking across the fire?

2. How does he practice to get this skill?

3. Explain how Khan thinks he can see without using his eyes.

4. Name 2 things that Khan does to practice his skill.

5.	At first, how many people believe Khan can see without his eyes?

6.	When can't Khan see without his eyes?

7.	Why could Khan see through cards?

8.	If you had Khan's power, what would you do?

VOCABULARY TO LEARN

worked up, somersaults, second-rate, persuade, overwhelming, grief, beyond the reach, an

outsider, change the course, an image, miracles

QUESTIONS

1.	What couldn't Dr. Cartwright do that night?

2.	Why did the doctor think Khan was valuable?

3.	How long did the doctor write that night?

4.	Why was the show cancelled?

5. What did Dr. Cartwright regret?

6. Why did the doctor think Khan died?

VOCABULARY TO LEARN

home and dry, bring it off, campaign, his bible, pantry, in twilight, the wick, absolutely blank,

fidgeting around, encased, throwing himself into, genuine enthusiasm, good sense, great

intensity, gloat over, fanatical, kept at it, at a stretch, exclusive

QUESTIONS

1. How could this story change Sugar's life?

2. Why wouldn't he want to tell anyone of his plan?

3. Who did Henry Sugar love most?

4. How long could he concentrate on his face on his first attempt?

5. After that day, how often did Henry practice?

6. What did Henry give up?

7. How much time did it take Henry to see his first card?

8. Why didn't he ever leave his flat?

9. How long did Henry want to take to be able to see the cards?

10. Why was Saturday night a good time to go to a casino?

CHAPTER 9-1 P.143-149

VOCABULARY TO LEARN

aristocracy, the curb, carved, sauntering, vulgar, wiped out of, polished, sleek, scurrying, a crescent moon, he's bust, a farce, vacant, perched, nimble fingers, absolute accuracy, stacked the chips, sarcastically, unbalanced him, staggering

QUESTIONS

1. Describe the casino Henry went to. (2)

2. What was special about rich men?

3. How does the reader know that Henry Sugar has changed?

4. What game did Henry play first?

5. How much money did he win?

6. Why didn't Henry win much money that night?

7. How does a player bust in blackjack?

8. What foolish thing had Henry done while playing blackjack?

VOCABULARY TO LEARN

tax-dodging, dishing out, the bulge, competent, fiction writer, wrap up this story, violated the

code, force of habit, arteries, veins, liver, kidneys, intestines, a blood clot, ultimately, apart

from that

QUESTIONS

1. Was the amount of money Henry won shocking to the casino?

2. What was Henry thinking about during his walk?

3. Why does the writer pause in the middle of this chapter?

4. How does this change the atmosphere in the chapter?

5. Why would the writer want to kill Henry Sugar?

6. What did the writer think would be an interesting way to kill Sugar?

7. What things were untrue in this story?

8. How would you describe Dahl's writing style?

VOCABULARY TO LEARN

melancholy, dawn upon, the process, outlook on life, acute revulsion, fluttered, shabby,

scrimmage, phenomenal, jostling, bellowed, a nuisance, blithering, an imbecile, pacing, corny,

sentimental

1. Why wasn't Henry excited about winning?

2. What did he do with the money that he had won?

3. Who was the first person to get Henry's money?

4. Why was the policeman so upset?

5. How did the policeman affect Henry?

6. In his plan, what couldn't Henry do?

7. What was the maximum amount of money Henry wanted to win each night?

8. Which part of his plan was the most important, and why?

CHAPTER 11	P.159-162

VOCABULARY TO LEARN

accountant, devised a system, a terrific effort, cautious, prudent, on the spur of the moment,

profit, operate out of, unattached bachelor, petty cash, tide you over, get cracking

1. Who was John Winston, and how long had Henry known him?

2. How did Henry prove his skill to John?

3. How does the reader know John was a cautious man?

4. Why did John want to work out of Switzerland?

5. How long did it take John to move?

6. How was Henry going to send money to John?

CHAPTER 12	P.162-163

VOCABULARY TO LEARN

as for, authorities, remittance, astonishing, his whereabouts

QUESTIONS

1. How often did Henry send money to John?

2. Why were the Monday deposits highest?

3.   How did John know where Henry was?

4.   What did each place that Henry went to have in common?

VOCABULARY TO LEARN

on the way, was bound to spread, the mob, a bellhop, tipping you off, thugs, revolving, sought

out, had no ties, enthusiastic, sideburns, diplomat, crusading, milking the casinos

QUESTIONS

1.   What trouble happened to Henry?

2.   How much money had Henry made since he started?

3.   Who saved Henry, and what was his reason?

4.   Because of this incident, how did Henry change his gambling system?

5.   What additional problems occurred because of this change in Henry's plan?

6.   How many people knew about Henry's plan?

7. How close were Max and Henry?

VOCABULARY TO LEARN

reference book, well-run, ignorance, with a view to, to merit, that needled me, enthralled,

shattered, word for word, by heart, staggering, a shot at, reveal, leak out

QUESTIONS

1. What was the most impressive thing about Henry Sugar's life?

2. Who is the "I" in this story?

3. Why did John want Henry's life story to be written?

4. How long did it take the writer to want to write Henry's life story?

5. How do we know that Henry was no longer interested in money for himself?

6. Why didn't the writer write about the stories in the casino?

7. Why didn't John want Henry's real name to be revealed?

---

8. What was the best part of this story?

Grammar Focus Section

GRAMMAR FOCUS 1

All of the sentences below have mistakes. You must correct the sentences, and make them **PERFECT**.

1. When I buy a furniture, I paid for them cash.

2. If I will eat a orange, I will peel a peel.

3. Even if the sun is farther away, it heat the Earth.

4. Whenever I studied in French, I use to be feeling a stress.

5. None of my friend don't like to play skiing.

6. All of people in this building doesn't own a helicopter made by China.

7. Neither my brother or my sister have a gold, shiny, small coin.

8. Unless you don't have a money, you can't buy a rice.

9. Before I went here today, I did met my friend brothers mother.

10. On Christmas, I was opened much present to Hana.

GRAMMAR FOCUS 2

All of the sentences below have mistakes. You must correct the sentences, and make them **PERFECT**.

1. I saw a men fell down his motorcycle last morning.

2. Playing a piano is funner than play computer game.

3. I want a plenty of hairs at my head, so I am little sad.

4. I occasionally am boring when I watch the television.

5. The city what I borned is call Wawa.

6. I accustomed to drive my car in winter road.

7. He look he will going to cry, and I don't know why.

8. A number of the childs in Canada has the only one parents.

9. Besides speak the English, I can speak also French.

10. By the time I will go back to home, I will eat lunch.

GRAMMAR FOCUS 3

All of the sentences below have mistakes. You must correct the sentences, and make them PERFECT.

1. I wish I can fly into the space and land in a moon.

_____

2. Despite cold weather today, I hope I could play a snowball fight.

_____

3. Each of my friend eat a turkey at Christmas day.

_____

4. I forgot studying my homework day before the yesterday.

_____

5. I think I sing song good, but the others doesn't.

_____

6. I talk slower when I teach, but I talk fastly when I meet my friend.

_____

7. You had better to drive slow when it snowy.

_____

8. My mom yesterday might have ate sandwich and a apple.

_____

9. You have got take a medicine, otherwise, you will feel sickly.

_____

10. Only if you are nice I will help your homework.

_____

GRAMMAR FOCUS 4

All of the sentences below have mistakes. You must correct the sentences, and make them **PERFECT**.

1. I bought several of tangerines at one of store near my home.

_____

2. He said he prefer hamburger than pizza.

_____

3. I went to a school since 2003 in Tokyo.

_____

4. I studied 2 hours and half so far.

_____

5. I don't have no friend in the Cuba, nevertheless, I won't go their.

_____

6. I am fond in read a book at the night before I go to a bed.

_____

7. This table is made from wood, and I purchased them at Ikea.

_____

8. I read in the magazine that 51% of world population are girls.

_____

9. If I had time enough yesterday, I watched TV.

_____

10. If I didn't have a breakfast, I get always hungry during class.

_____

GRAMMAR FOCUS 5

All of the sentences below have mistakes. You must correct the sentences, and make them **PERFECT**.

1. Whoever help to me, I will give to them a big, new, nice present.

   _____

2. I hate the bugs, but one times, I ate bug by a mistake.

   _____

3. He was a dumb when he was grade 4, so I don't play with him.

   _____

4. I wrote letters for my friend because he had operation in his heart.

   _____

5. Police found out who was the robber, so the robber went in jail.

   _____

6. I borrowed 2 books to the MeowMeow Library, but two books were bored.

   _____

7. I met real Santa on a roof of my home, and he was a lot shocked.

   _____

8. I never don't play Nintendo Switch, but I am wanting to.

   _____

9. I put off to do my homework because my grandma visited to me.

   _____

10. I want drink same juice like you.

   _____

GRAMMAR FOCUS 6

All of the sentences below have mistakes. You must correct the sentences, and make them **PERFECT**.

1. While I went to upstairs, I tripped on ball, and fell down stairs.

2. Your shoe look like ugly, so how many money did you spend on it.

3. When I go school, I put on an uniform, and put books onto my bag.

4. It is a bathroom besides this room, but don't go into there.

5. I haven't a puppy, but I want it for Christmas present.

6. If I had puppy, I could walk with her, and playing.

7. My mom make me to clean in my room.

8. She tells sometimes to me that my room smell like wet socks.

9. The twin resembles every other, but their clothes is differently.

10. At the last day in the year, almost of everybody go to temple.

GRAMMAR FOCUS 7

All of the sentences below have mistakes. You must correct the sentences, and make them PERFECT.

1. While the vacation, we are rested well.

    _____

2. I did not to understand my teacher question , so I quiet.

    _____

3. Nobody can't eat hamburger and swimming at same time.

    _____

4. My sister have much talents, so she has popular.

    _____

5. My father give it to me a blue nice jacket I am wearing.

    _____

6. My computer was costed me $1000, and it was in sale.

    _____

7. I'm might to play my friend by 5 o'clock.

    _____

8. I will enter sing contest because my sing is beautifully.

    _____

9. People are not used to live in warmly weather these day.

    _____

10. Did you know who was invented TV?

    _____

GRAMMAR FOCUS 8

All of the sentences below have mistakes. You must correct the sentences, and make them **PERFECT**.

1. This spagetties are tasting very good. Who made that?

2. Every frogs have for legs, and some frog have poisonous.

3. At Halloween day, we can find many candy and chocolates.

4. That nicely shoes are Hana, so don't touch it.

5. Most of people in Japan eat the rice everyday.

6. The Italy, expensive, red car is very cuty. Who's car is that?

7. Almost people dislike to do a homework

8. You must go school, even if it is snowing much today.

9. She running slow because she is hurted on her leg.

10. Your room is a big messy, so you better cleaning up it.

GRAMMAR FOCUS 9

All of the sentences below have mistakes. You must correct the sentences, and make them **PERFECT**.

1. As soon as he was woke up, and he washed his hand.

2. He always were late in class, so not anymore.

3. Mine computer was made by Japan on the factory.

4. She don't enjoy to playing soccer with me and hers brother.

5. Studying the French is boring than studying Maths.

6. They is best student in a class because they study hardly.

7. A apple is deliciouser then bananas from Philippines.

8. I walk slow, but my friend get angry to me.

9. In morning, I eat sometime bread in kitchen with a jam.

10. At top of the Keira Mountain, it is a coffee shop.

GRAMMAR FOCUS 10

All of the sentences below have mistakes. You must correct the sentences, and make them **PERFECT**.

1. Even though I am Japanese, but I speak Japanese.

_____

2. First time I met my the best friend, he was played the tennis.

_____

3. When weather is a humid, many of people drink a water.

_____

4. After she will finishes her exams, she plans going to a trip.

_____

5. By the time I had come to here, I ate the breakfast.

_____

6. While he read a book, he eat sandwich of ham.

_____

7. I lived in home since I am young, and I live there now still.

_____

8. I lend a books from library last time I went to there.

_____

9. I am thinking that whenever I ill, I take a medicine.

_____

10. I saw a lady talked a tiger last week. It was danger.

_____

GRAMMAR FOCUS 11

1. Although weathers are nice, I played outside all the day long.

   _____

2. Some peoples never have been to outside their country.

   _____

3. I am disappoint sometimes when students fail test.

   _____

4. Every times I am boring, I try to make by myself more happy.

   _____

5. I really like you new, leather, beautiful, long jacket.

   _____

6. None of student in this class have bad personality.

   _____

7. Every boys and girls and monkeys usually are nicely to older people.

   _____

8. I can't imagine to eat a bug, but some of people do it.

   _____

9. Rice grows by farmers.

   _____

10. She made me to cry because she hitted me with chopstick.

   _____

GRAMMAR FOCUS 12

All of the sentences below have mistakes. You must correct the sentences, and make them **PERFECT**.

1. Do you mind to open a window in this room to me?

_____

2. How much long you will live in here?

_____

3. Why you can't doing always your homeworks yourself?

_____

4. How often do she go to shopping with hers friend?

_____

5. I don't know who are you, so please tell to me your name.

_____

6. I would like know what kind of ice-creams he does like.

_____

7. People on that bus must to be hot because all windows are up.

_____

8. Eating the lettuces are well for your healthy.

_____

9. One of house near to my home have a plenty of window.

_____

10. Each of my book are interested.

_____

GRAMMAR FOCUS 13

All of the sentences below have mistakes. You must correct the sentences, and make them **PERFECT**.

1. He got punish by teacher because cheating in tests.

_____

2. I want to invent the robot that could washing a dishes fastly.

_____

3. All of student failed a test, even a best student in class.

_____

4. I saw she laughed a lot when she watched the man fell down.

_____

5. He don't like play the sports with them boys.

_____

6. First time he meet his teacher, he was quiet too much.

_____

7. I asked to she that she can skiing very good.

_____

8. I am guessing you interested at the soccer.

_____

9. She trips to Osaka twice times a month.

_____

10. It is many kind of tree in a park close my home.

_____

GRAMMAR FOCUS 14

All of the sentences below have mistakes. You must correct the sentences, and make them **PERFECT**.

1. If I am you, I will practice golfing almost always.

2. The last time I visited to the Germany, I have good time.

3. I went to German on airplane, and it took for me 10 hours.

4. He have a circle face, and a long leg.

5. Whenever I plays drums very loud, my neighbourhood complain.

6. Every other days, she goes to shopping for buying a bread.

7. She was being sad about she lost her car's keys.

8. I hope my hair is long than you.

9. Megan wish she can drive more quicker than me.

10. He did good in the test, so his mom buys for him a new game.

GRAMMAR FOCUS 15

All of the sentences below have mistakes. You must correct the sentences, and make them PERFECT.

1. I forgot almost to writing about my holiday at Canada.

2. Please call to me whenever you are needing some helps.

3. I have many problem of my car, and I want to change them.

4. The robber caught by police early at morning.

5. Most surprised thing was that the robber was the girl.

6. Me and my friend tired of play the computer games on internet.

7. The cars need the gas to move, but gas is cheap not so much.

8. The stuffs for making cake is sugars, butters, flours, etcs.

9. Live in Hawaii must be a fun because it is beaches everywhere.

10. That Japanese, small car is same size to my car.

GRAMMAR FOCUS 16

All of the sentences below have mistakes. You must correct the sentences, and make them **PERFECT**.

1. His foot smell a fish. Maybe he is fisherman.

2. He is looking as if he woke up just today morning.

3. He got trouble at his class by no reason.

4. Even though he was studied lot, but he got F at the test.

5. The last year, he dreamed to live on a tree in Amazon Jungle.

6. My teacher gave me many homework, and I don't finish them yet.

7. I heard a rumor during I was studying on last Friday.

8. I buyed this dictionary so that I learn the English.

9. Because of weather, golf tournament called up.

10. I borned at hospital in a quite small city.

Prepositions Section

PREPOSITIONS 1

Write a proper preposition for each sentence. Sometimes, there is more than one answer. Also, prepositions are used in idioms. These phrasal verbs must be memorized.

1. When I moved _____ my new home, I left a nice apartment _____ the 5th floor.

2. _____ January, but not _____ January 1st, the wind blows strongly _____ the east.

3. _____ Christmas, I opened _____ gifts wrapped _____ Christmas paper.

4. If you are addicted _____ playing games _____-line, you should throw _____ your computer.

5. I am bothered _____ people who speak _____ their friends loudly _____ their cell-phones.

6. I need to cut _____ _____ sugar because I think my stomach will blow _____.

7. _____ top _____ Mount Fuji, there is a hotel made _____ Mr. Soto.

8. My grandma was a witness _____ a tornado _____ least 3 times in her life.

9. I was just _____ to drop _____ my friend's house when he sent an e-mail _____ me.

10. Just _____ you and me, I don't like shopping _____ all.

11. It is _____ the law to steal _____ banks, or to take things _____ paying.

12. My friend asked me _____ to his home _____ dinner, so I was thankful _____ him.

13. The movie will come _____ _____ weeks, and I am looking _____ to that.

14. He was knocked _____, but he came _____ very quickly.

15. I can't come _____ _____ the answer _____ your question.

PREPOSITIONS 2

1. The movie finishes _____ 9pm, so can you pick me _____ when it is _____?

2. Can you help me blow _____ these balloons? I am all _____ _____ power.

3. I am furious _____ getting an F _____ my test. Usually Math is easy _____ me.

4. He is hopeless _____ making food, so he needs to brush _____ _____ his cooking.

5. Who is responsible _____ drinking _____ all _____ my juice?

6. _____ Boxing Day, many people waited _____ a line to buy things _____ sale.

7. _____ hot summer nights, people swim _____ water to cool _____.

8. People play _____ balls _____ the park _____ the end _____ my street _____ summer.

9. _____ Hokkaido Island _____ the north, you can find homes made _____ ice.

10. When people sit _____ the front _____ my car, they are banned _____ eating.

11. There is a pen made _____ China _____ the corner _____ this room.

12. Hang _____ your coat _____ the back _____ the room.

13. There is a demand _____ oil _____ the world, so the price _____ oil has gone _____.

14. What is your reason _____ being late? Did you sleep _____, or forget _____ our meeting?

15. There has been a rise _____ the temperature due _____ global warming.

PREPOSITIONS 3

Fill in the blank
Write a proper preposition for each sentence. Sometimes, there is more than one answer. Also, prepositions are used in idioms. These phrasal verbs must be memorized.

1. Did you ever find _____ what the cause _____ your sickness was?

2. I was _____ an accident yesterday, and there was much damage _____ my car.

3. After I got an invitation _____ the Queen's party, I accepted _____ once.

4. Hurry _____ and make _____ your mind. What is the solution _____ my question?

5. The police asked me if I had a relationship _____ the guy _____ Cuba _____ the 20th floor.

6. I made contact _____ my uncle who I hadn't seen _____ ages.

7. I pay _____ my rent _____ check, not _____ cash.

8. I was walking _____ Odori Street when I found a diamond _____ chance.

9. Romeo and Juliet is set _____ Italy, and was written _____ Shakespeare _____ the 16th century.

10. _____ dusk, I sometimes go _____ _____ a walk _____ Hana _____ an hour.

11. _____ my opinion, translating English _____ Japanese is not easy _____ young children.

12. My building was _____ fire, so I jumped _____ my balcony and _____ the ground.

13. Bus drivers went _____ strike because _____ a lack _____ money.

14. It was stupid _____ me to believe _____ ghosts when I was young.

15. I am kind _____ people who take care _____ my dog when I leave _____ vacation.

PREPOSITIONS 4

1. My sister is a pushover _____ chocolate, so she is happy when I buy some _____ her.

2. I am not fond _____ mushrooms _____ all, so I avoid eating them _____ all cost.

3. I have respect _____ people who are dedicated _____ their jobs.

4. _____ average, Canadians eat _____ 50 hot-dogs a year.

5. I don't like to comment _____ things I don't know _____.

6. Basically, I prefer bananas _____ apples _____ summer.

7. It's dangerous _____ people to stand _____ his shoes because _____ the smell.

8. I was confused _____ what you said _____ me _____ the car last night.

9. What are you angry _____? Your life is great, you are _____ shape, and you are smart _____ Isaac Newton.

10. Young children depend _____ their parents _____ everything.

11. Billy and Mary split _____ last week because Billy told a lie _____ Mary.

12. My mom burst _____ my room, yelled _____ me to wake-_____, then turned _____ the light.

13. Babies act _____ when they are tired, so parents need to care _____ them.

14. I agree _____ your plan _____ go _____ a diet, but can you do it _____ yourself?

15. I will begin this class _____ explaining the vocabulary _____ chapter 3.

PREPOSITIONS 5

1. Dogs bark _____ people who stray _____ their homes late _____ the afternoon.

2. I didn't study _____ the test. _____ the way, what are you doing _____ your birthday?

3. The house burned _____ because a young boy was playing _____ fire.

4. Snow was building _____ _____ my home because _____ the snowstorm.

5. I want to be fluent _____ Spanish, but I can't catch _____ to what my teacher is saying.

6. You must choose _____ the truck made _____ metal, and the car made _____ Germany.

7. You aren't allowed _____ cut _____ the grass _____ this park.

8. The man died _____ a heart attack. He always sat _____ his sofa, and he was _____ _____ shape.

9. The man disappeared _____ a trace, so the police are looking _____ him _____ dogs.

10. People can't do _____ computers, so they are reliant _____ them.

11. The coach drew _____ a plan to score a goal _____ the goalie.

12. She took all _____ the money, and went to a casino _____ bus.

13. _____ dawn, I put _____ my jacket, picked _____ the phone, and called _____ a taxi.

14. People are faced _____ many challenges _____ their lives.

15. I'm too busy, so I don't think I can finish my work _____ time.

PREPOSITIONS 6

1. This is the best hamburger I've ever eaten. It is a cut _____ other hamburgers.

2. When I feel _____, I go _____ a walk _____ an hour.

3. I sold my car _____ a good price. I got $10,000 _____ it.

4. Stop fooling _____ and grow _____. You are always acting _____ a baby.

5. I don't like your idea, but I will go _____ _____ your plan anyways.

6. I know you are angry _____ me, but just sit _____ and listen _____ me.

7. Cats hide _____ dogs because dogs chase _____ cats.

8. _____ Friday night, my friend helped me _____ my computer because it broke _____.

9. All people hope _____ happiness because it is important _____ people.

10. I was hurt _____ your punch, so I will take revenge _____ you.

11. He is close _____ his mom, but doesn't keep _____ contact _____ his dad.

12. I can't be involved _____ you. Leave me _____ _____ your plans.

13. The police are looking _____ the robbery _____ the bank.

14. You look stressed _____. You need to loosen _____.

15. I moved _____ _____ my home yesterday, and moved _____ my new home today.

PREPOSITIONS 7

1. I was named _____ my grandfather because my mom really looked _____ _____ him.

2. There is a need _____ fresh water _____ Africa, especially _____ the winter season.

3. My neighbour is driving me crazy. I have to put _____ _____ his singing all the time.

4. Do you have any questions _____ me _____ the test tomorrow?

5. Poor people live _____ money, and my teacher lives _____ hair _____ his head.

6. When she saw a wild tiger, she ran _____ _____ the tiger, but the tiger was faster.

7. What did you say _____ me? Speak _____ and talk _____ a clear voice.

8. Would you like to share your lunch _____ me? I forgot my lunch _____ my home.

9. I think you are great _____ dancing. Why don't you dance _____ me _____ your free time?

10. People say my feet smell _____ flowers growing _____ a mountain _____ summer.

11. I usually spend time _____ my computer or _____ my friends.

12. I need to stop _____ the store to pick _____ some juice _____ the party.

13. I want a new hobby. I think I'll take _____ painting. Maybe I'm talented _____ it.

14. I can't think _____ what to buy Hana _____ her birthday _____ July.

15. Many people think I had surgery _____ my face because I look _____ an actor, but it is not true

PREPOSITIONS 8

Fill in the blank
Write a proper preposition for each sentence. Sometimes, there is more than one answer. Also, prepositions are used in idioms. These phrasal verbs must be memorized.

1. I got information _____ a book _____ dinosaurs _____ the library.

2. When I work late _____ night, I often can't eat dinner _____ my family.

3. The bad man was arrested _____ the police and put _____ jail _____ life.

4. I will give you my phone number, so write it _____ _____ your book.

5. When I get bad news, I often think _____ that news _____ a long time.

6. Airplanes fly _____ clouds _____ the sky _____ Canada _____ Asia.

7. I get _____ _____ people who care _____ animals.

8. When I cook, and chop _____ vegetables grown _____ Japan _____ farms.

9. I am growing tired _____ looking _____ the snow _____ the ground.

10. I called _____ my friend yesterday, but he didn't hear me _____ all.

11. I was injured _____ a car accident, and I got a cut _____ my arm.

12. You must keep _____ trying hard, and never give _____, or else you will fail.

13. My eyes are bad. I can't make _____ what kind _____ bird that is.

14. _____ one hand, I like to eat _____, but _____ the other hand, it is expensive.

15. I have a moustache, but I will shave it _____ tomorrow.

PREPOSITIONS 9

1. The fire, caused _____ the little boy, burned _____ the house.

2. His mother was so angry _____ him that she hit him _____ the leg.

3. The boy went _____ a hospital, and had surgery _____ his knee.

4. _____ that time, the boy was afraid _____ his mom.

5. So, the boy moved _____ _____ his grandmother.

6. She lived _____ Lake Road, _____ the 4th floor _____ a building.

7. They lived _____ each other _____ many years.

8. _____ last, the boy graduated _____ the University _____ Harvard.

9. He got a masters degree _____ medicine, and was the top student _____ his class.

10. The boy decided _____ working _____ Africa.

11. _____ poor countries, there is a need _____ good doctors.

12. One day, the boy was _____ to get _____ the plane when something bad happened _____ him.

13. He saw his mother begging _____ money _____ front _____ a bathroom.

14. When she saw him, she yelled _____ him, but the boy didn't pay attention _____ her.

15. _____ the air, _____ the Atlantic ocean, _____ his seat, the boy began to cry.

PREPOSITIONS 10

Fill in the blank
Write a proper preposition for each sentence. Sometimes, there is more than one answer. Also, prepositions are used in idioms. These phrasal verbs must be memorized.

1. I woke _____ _____ my bed _____ 5am _____ the morning.

2. I picked _____ the phone, and ordered a pizza _____ Pizza Hurt.

3. I came here _____ bus because my car broke _____ _____ a river.

4. I paid _____ the car _____ cash, not _____ credit, or _____ a loan.

5. A robber broke _____ a bank, and stole all _____ the money.

6. So, the police are looking _____ that man who stole money _____ the bank

7. Green tea _____ Asia is good _____ people's health.

8. I was happy _____ passing the test _____ March 13.

9. _____ summer, I will camp _____ my friends _____ a tent.

10. Button _____ your jacket, and put _____ your hat.

11. I read a story _____ China _____ a magazine, but I got bored _____ it.

12. I want to heat _____ my food, so I will put it _____ my microwave _____ 3 minutes.

13. Can you look _____ my report _____ I hand it _____?

14. Just _____ you and me, I don't like him _____ all.

15. I am fed _____ _____ listening _____ this song. Turn it _____.

PREPOSITIONS 11

Fill in the blank
Write a proper preposition for each sentence. Sometimes, there is more than one answer. Also, prepositions are used in idioms. These phrasal verbs must be memorized.

1. _____ the afternoon, I like to sleep _____ my bed _____ my pyjamas _____ 2 hours.

2. When I turn _____ my computer, I sit _____ my chair and drink coffee.

3. I sometimes argue _____ baseball _____ Hana.

4. Math is easy _____ you, but hard _____ me. I can't catch _____ _____ all.

5. My pen is made _____ plastic, _____ a man _____ China _____ .

6. _____ last, my friend arrived _____ my home _____ dinner.

7. The letter B is _____ A and C, and banana starts _____ the letter B.

8. I am different _____ you _____ many ways.

9. My grandma cared _____ me when I was _____ elementary school.

10. When I wait _____ line _____ the bank, I watch movies _____ my phone.

11. I weigh _____ 80 kg, so I must go _____ a diet.

12. _____ the chairs _____ my office, I like mine the most.

13. I am so _____ with my project that I can't hand it _____ _____ time.

14. Hana put _____ a fire _____ my kitchen _____ water yesterday.

15. That book was written _____ a lady who works _____ free.

PREPOSITIONS 12

Fill in the blank
Write a proper preposition for each sentence. Sometimes, there is more than one answer. Also, prepositions are used in idioms. These phrasal verbs must be memorized.

1. Vegetables are good _____ your health, so eat _____ least 3 every day.

2. There are many trees _____ the bottom _____ the hill _____ Montreal Island.

3. They always argue _____ stupid things. They should break _____.

4. People who are sick should stay _____ bed, and wash their hands _____ soap.

5. _____ summer, many birds search _____ food, and build nests _____ sticks.

6. I am allergic _____ fish that swim _____ rivers.

7. I woke _____ _____ half _____ 6 this morning.

8. I lived _____ Korea _____ 6 years before I moved _____ to Canada.

9. We have been studying _____ 3 pm _____ our chairs _____ this building.

10. I met Hana _____ the first time _____ top _____ a mountain.

11. A monkey jumped _____ my back, and hit me _____ the arm.

12. That house is _____ sale, but I am not interested _____ it _____ the least.

13. _____ Pizza Hut, I saw a man slip _____ a piece of pepperoni, and fall _____.

14. What's the matter _____ you? What are you crying _____? Cheer _____.

15. Lunch is _____ breakfast and dinner, and is usually _____ 12 o'clock.

PREPOSITIONS 13

Fill in the blank
Write a proper preposition for each sentence. Sometimes, there is more than one answer. Also, prepositions are used in idioms. These phrasal verbs must be memorized.

1. I like to play games _____ fun _____ my computer.

2. I bought my radio _____ cash _____ Yodobashi _____ sale.

3. The dark sky is clearing _____, so let's start _____ the BBQ.

4. Be careful _____ that bomb. You might drop it _____ the floor and blow us _____.

5. _____ the middle _____ the hill, there is a bear that lives _____ a cave _____ itself.

6. The boy saved _____ some money _____ a new bike.

7. Stars _____ the sky shiny brightly _____ the ocean.

8. Talking _____ a phone _____ a long time is not good.

9. What do you want _____ dessert? I have ice cream made _____ goat milk.

10. I don't get _____ _____ that guy. We are not friends.

11. The World Cup _____ 2018 was played _____ Russia

12. The car was moving _____ the highway _____ 100km an hour.

13. I have a pain _____ my leg. Why did you hit me _____ the stick?

14. This book will prepare you _____ many tests.

15. There is a window _____ the back _____ this room made _____ me.

PREPOSITIONS 14

Fill in the blank
Write a proper preposition for each sentence. Sometimes, there is more than one answer. Also, prepositions are used in idioms. These phrasal verbs must be memorized.

1. The building has been _____ construction _____ December.

2. The picnic was called _____ and rescheduled _____ Sunday.

3. He got away _____ stealing an apple _____ a farm.

4. When you study _____ a library, turn _____ your cell phone.

5. I was born _____ March, _____ an elevator _____ the 2ⁿᵈ floor _____ a hospital.

6. _____ the internet, people play games _____ other people.

7. Bees are attracted _____ flowers _____ forests.

8. What is the difference _____ Chinese and Korean people?

9. The winner _____ the game will go _____ the tournament _____ April.

10. It took me 10 days to get _____ my cold. It was hard to recover _____ it.

11. I like to sleep _____ _____ Sundays.

12. I saw a ghost _____ the first time _____ my life yesterday.

13. _____ midnight, I put _____ my coat, and went _____ a walk _____ my dog.

14. Fireworks were invented _____ the Chinese _____ the 3ʳᵈ century.

15. _____ last, I finished my report _____ bugs.

PREPOSITIONS 15

Fill in the blank
Write a proper preposition for each sentence. Sometimes, there is more than one answer. Also, prepositions are used in idioms. These phrasal verbs must be memorized.

1. I am not a fan _____ fighting _____ classrooms.

2. Your feet are _____ your socks and look _____ hands.

3. Don't throw that piece _____ cake _____ me.

4. _____ a short time, we will say goodbye. Don't be sad _____ that.

5. The bad student never pays attention _____ the teacher, so he gets punished _____ that.

6. I liked her _____ the beginning, but she never chatted _____ me.

7. I am _____ favour _____ giving students homework, but they are _____ that idea.

8. The meteor fell _____ space, and _____ the ocean.

9. There is a café _____ the top _____ Asashiyama Mountain, but it's closed _____ winter.

10. _____ her holiday, Cindy went _____ a picnic _____ a beach.

11. When he walked _____ the door, he tripped _____ a bicycle, and fell _____.

12. If a book is upside _____, people can't read it _____ all.

13. Today, I feel _____, so I might cry _____ loud _____ a baby.

14. If you have hicc_____s, hold your breath _____ 1 minute.

15. Many colours look good _____ me. _____ example, brown.

PREPOSITIONS 16

Fill in the blank
Write a proper preposition for each sentence. Sometimes, there is more than one answer. Also, prepositions are used in idioms. These phrasal verbs must be memorized.

---

1. I ran _____ _____ sugar, so I bought some _____ sale _____ a dollar.

2. I think skiing _____ hills is difficult _____ some people.

3. I hate seeing the words, "Game _____" when I play games _____ a computer.

4. I live _____ _____ a library that is closed _____ weekends.

5. I put a painting _____ my face _____ the wall today, but Hana took it _____ quickly.

6. When I am fed _____ _____ doing work, I go _____ a walk.

7. I bought this _____ a man _____ Mexico _____ a good price.

8. Hold _____. I have never been _____ Mexico _____ my life.

9. Let's swim _____ the middle _____ the lake.

10. That song sounds _____ a song _____ AKB47.

11. _____ the army, I wasn't allowed to lean _____ walls.

12. I need your help _____ a minute. I can't figure _____ this problem.

13. Last April, _____ a Thursday night, the temperature went _____ zero, so water froze.

14. I sometimes picked _____ my sister. Then she tried to fight _____ me.

15. We've studied _____ years. _____ now, you should be good _____ English.

Articles Section

ARTICLES 1

At _____ end of _____ week, I always go to _____ Homac with _____ friend of mine. However, last

week, my friend, who is _____ policeman, called me to tell me _____ bad news. He had to go on _____

secret mission to _____ Forest Park, and meet _____ man who worked for _____ Chinese. My friend told

me he was _____ spy, and that _____ Chinese man was also _____ spy who was secretly working for

_____ RCMP, Canada's secret _____ police. For _____ first time in my life, I was worried, so I told my

friend, "_____ Next time you have to go somewhere, I can help." So, my friend asked me if I could drive him to

_____ park, and I said yes. We went to _____ park, and we met _____ Chinese man. _____ Chinese man

gave my friend _____ plenty of _____ pictures of famous places around _____ world. There were

pictures of _____ Gobi Desert, _____ Atlantic Ocean, _____ Philippines, _____ Mitsui Shopping Mall,

_____ Sun Life Building, and _____ Seoul National University. Also, he had pictures of _____ Vancouver

Airport, _____ Central Park in _____ New York, and _____ Lachine Canal. _____ Two men said goodbye,

and that was _____ last time I ever saw that man.

ARTICLES 2

_____ Olympics is _____ competition to see who can be _____ best in _____ world. Many

athletes from _____ Canada went by _____ airplane to _____ country of Italy, and they did very

well. _____ Canadians are good at _____ hockey and _____ skiing. On _____ TV, I saw many

people trying very hard to win _____ medal, but not all of _____ people won. I saw _____ German

skier fall down _____ mountain, and I think he was hurt, so _____ police took him to _____ hospital in _____ helicopter. _____ hospital is called _____ Pasta Hospital. After _____ German skier got better, he took _____ tour of Rome, and he saw many beautiful things. He went to _____ St. Tiramisu Square, _____ Roma River, _____ Bella Museum, _____ Spaghetti Stadium, and _____ Lira Park. In _____ park, he tripped over _____ rock, and hurt his body again. He went back to _____ same hospital, and is still there now.

ARTICLES 3

Fill in the blanks (a, an, the or X)
Articles are always used before nouns. Common singular nouns (i.e. a car, a chair, an apple) are the most common nouns to take articles. Proper nouns (i.e. The Hudson River) sometimes take the article THE, sometimes not. Non-counting nouns and plural nouns also take articles sometimes, if they are known to the speaker (i.e. The water in my glass is hot)

1. _____ Last time I went to _____ Aeon, I bought _____ rice.

2. _____ Nile Delta is close to _____ Sahara Desert.

3. _____ Pacific Ocean has many kinds of _____ sharks in it like _____ tiger shark.

4. I met Hana for _____ first time in _____ 2000 in _____ HSBC Building.

5. _____ University of McGill is on _____ Sherbrooke Street and is _____ top school in Canada.

6. This is _____ only pen I have, so it is _____ best pen I have. It is made by _____ Bic Company.

7. _____ Sony makes many _____ games for _____ kids under _____ age of 13.

8. _____ Elephant at _____ Granby Zoo can eat _____ lots of _____ food everyday.

9. _____ English have _____ nice accent, but it is hard to understand at _____ times.

10. I went to _____ school, then to _____ church, then to _____ work, then went to _____ bed.

11. I will travel _____ east this summer. I want to go to _____ east coast.

12. From _____ beginning, I knew that I couldn't play _____ guitar.

13. On _____ last day of _____ month, I will buy _____ Subaru Forrester.

14. At _____ end of _____ WWII, _____ Germans had difficult lives.

15. _____ Most Arabs don't like to eat _____ rabbit in _____ restaurant.

ARTICLES 4

While I was camping in _____ Sherwood Forest I met _____ man who was holding _____ gun in

his _____ hand. I asked _____ man what he was doing with _____ gun, and he suddenly had

_____ frown on his _____ face. He told me _____ crazy story about his life during _____

last 24 hours. When he woke up yesterday, he was on _____ boat called _____ Fisherman, _____

famous boat from _____ Canary Islands. When he got out of _____ bed, he felt _____ sick, so he

sat on _____ floor. He couldn't remember how he got on _____ boat. When he went to _____ top

of _____ boat, he couldn't find anyone, so he called _____ police. However, before _____

policeman could help him, _____ large boat started to shoot at him. _____ man started to sail

_____ boat. He went to _____ Suez Canal, _____ Beaver Lake, _____ East Sea, _____

Grand Rapids, _____ Sandy Beach, and _____ Yucatan Peninsula. _____ Man got off _____

boat, and ran into _____ Sherwood Forest.

ARTICLES 5

_____ Longest wall in _____ world is in _____ China. It is called _____ Great Wall of China,

and it was built _____ long time ago. _____ Chinese began building it in _____ 7th century BC, and

finished it in _____ 17th century AD. It was finished in _____ Qin Dynasty, and some people say it was built to stop attackers or ghosts from entering China. China had enemies in _____ north, called _____ Huns.

_____ wall goes through _____ Gobi Desert, and it was built from _____ east to _____ west.

_____ Western part of _____ wall passes along _____ Yellow River. Other things to see in China are

_____ Silk Road, _____ highway that joined _____ east to _____ west. _____ Mogao

Caves are beautiful caves filled with statues of _____ Buddha. In _____ center of _____ Beijing, we

can see _____ Forbidden City, called Gu Gong in _____ Chinese. It was _____ imperial palace

during _____ Ming and Qing dynasties. _____ Stone Forest is one of _____ most important

attractions of _____ Yunnan Province. China seems to be _____ amazing place to visit, so I'd really like to go there

in _____ airplane with _____ friend of mine.

ARTICLES 6

Fill in the blanks (a, an, the or X)
Articles are always used before nouns. Common singular nouns (i.e. a car, a chair, an apple) are the most common nouns to take articles. Proper nouns (i.e. The Hudson River) sometimes take the article THE, sometimes not. Non-counting nouns and plural nouns also take articles sometimes, if they are known to the speaker (i.e. The water in my glass is hot)

There was _____ boy named Robby, and he had _____ stress about moving to _____ Laos. _____

Problem was, he didn't know anything about _____ country. He had won _____ 1st prize in _____ contest at

_____ C.U. Later High School in _____ province of Gifu. _____ winner of _____ contest could study

in _____ Laos for _____ year. He went to _____ Sayonara Airport by _____ taxi in _____

morning. He wore his _____ best suit, and said goodbye to his _____ family. On his _____ way to

_____ country, he flew over _____ Hawaiin Islands in _____ USA. He saw many beautiful places.

_____ Maui Beach has beautiful _____ sand. _____ Coconut Bridge is very long. _____ Mua-mua

Mountain has _____ volcano on it that is _____ second largest mountain in _____ Hawaii. _____

First time he saw _____ Snake River, he was surprised because it was such _____ lovely river. He saw many other

fantastic things, and after _____ few hours, the plane landed at _____ Wattay International Airport.

ARTICLES 7

There was _____ girl named Sandy who had _____ dream to make _____ best gum in _____

universe. She lived in _____ quiet mansion on _____ Maple Road with her _____ parents. Her

room was on _____ 5th floor of _____ very big home. She lived next to _____ Great Wall of China,

and around _____ wall was _____ fantastic garden. Sandy always picked things from _____ garden,

and used them in _____ gum she made. _____ Girl had _____ brother named Larry, and he always

tasted _____ gum _____ girl made. Every _____ other day, Sandy went to _____ garden to

pick different kinds of _____ plants, _____ fruit, _____ vegetables, and even _____ bugs to

make her gum. _____ First gum she made was _____ gum made of rose thorns, two strawberries, and

_____ mosquito's eyeball. When Larry chewed _____ gum for _____ first time, it tasted good.

However, 1 minute later, something strange happened to him. He turned into _____ bird, and flew to many

strange places. He flew over _____ Swiss Alps and _____ Purple Port. Then, he landed on _____

Empire State Building, where he could see _____ Brooklyn Bridge, _____ Hudson River, and _____

Quiet Library. Finally, on _____ last day of April, he went back home. Sandy was such _____ happy girl

because her brother finally came home. She never made gum ever again.

ARTICLES 8

When _____ president of Korea took _____ navy boat around _____ Korean Peninsula, he was

very surprised. On one island, he saw _____ tree which was growing _____ rice. When he got off

_____ boat, and went to _____ Yellow Beach, he walked into _____ Green Forest and started to

take _____ rice that was on _____ tree. Suddenly, _____ old woman with _____ dog and

_____ squirrel on her head screamed at _____ president, "What are you doing on _____ Circle Island?" _____ President laughed and said, "This is my _____ island, and I can do whatever I want." Then _____ lady laughed, and ran to _____ top of _____ Tall Tower, and quietly spoke to _____ squirrel. _____ Thousands of squirrels started to climb up all _____ trees in _____ Green Forest, and began to throw _____ lots of _____ things at _____ president. The president wanted to stay, but he couldn't, so he ran back to _____ boat that was in _____ East Sea, and then sailed _____ West towards _____ Port of Inchon. When _____ president became _____ old man, he sometimes thought about _____ time he went to _____ Circle Island. He never went back to _____ island, but sometimes he thinks about that _____ very special _____ rice tree.

ARTICLES 9

Fill in the blanks (a, an, the or X)
Articles are always used before nouns. Common singular nouns (i.e. a car, a chair, an apple) are the most common nouns to take articles. Proper nouns (i.e. The Hudson River) sometimes take the article THE, sometimes not. Non-counting nouns and plural nouns also take articles sometimes, if they are known to the speaker (i.e. The water in my glass is hot)

Candy Land

In _____ galaxy called _____ Choco Galaxy, there was _____ planet named _____ Kandi. It was _____ extremely beautiful place. On _____ planet, there lived _____ only one man, and so he called himself _____ King Kandi _____ Lucky. He was such _____ lonely man. So he decided to have _____ contest, _____ candy eating contest. _____ Next day, 12 373 people entered _____ contest, all wanting to win _____ 1st prize. People from _____ other planets all arrived at _____ Kandi Airport in _____ UFOs, and all of _____ people stayed at _____ Kandi Hotel near _____ Kandi Pond and _____ Kandi Jungle. On _____ day of _____ contest, each person entered _____ Kandi Hall near _____ Kandi Stadium, and each person was given _____ bowl of _____ candy. _____ King Kandi held _____ whistle in his _____ mouth, and when he blew _____ whistle, everyone started to eat _____ candy in _____ bowls. After half _____ hour, _____ king blew his whistle again, and everyone stopped. After checking, _____ king knew who

_____ winner was. He got onto _____ stage in _____ hall, and said, "Thank you all for coming to Kandi, and I hope you had _____ wonderful time visiting my beautiful planet. _____ Person who finished _____ 1st is _____ only person who ate all of _____ candy. There is _____ only one person who did this, and this person will get _____ secret prize. Her name is Malia, and she is _____ 14 year old girl who studies at _____ TOEM School on planet Maruyama. Please come here and get your prize." Malai ran like _____ rabbit up to _____ stage, and was so happy that she hit _____ king in _____ arm. _____ King Kandi handed her _____ prize, which was in _____ orange box, and everyone became silent. Malia opened _____ box, took it out, and showed it to everyone. It was _____ picture, _____ very ugly picture of King Kandi. Everyone was disappointed, especially Malia, so they all left right away. At least they all got to eat delicious candy.

ARTICLES 10

Fill in the blanks (a, an, the or X)
Articles are always used before nouns. Common singular nouns (i.e. a car, a chair, an apple) are the most common nouns to take articles. Proper nouns (i.e. The Hudson River) sometimes take the article THE, sometimes not. Non-counting nouns and plural nouns also take articles sometimes, if they are known to the speaker (i.e. The water in my glass is hot)

1. At _____ first, I wasn't interested in _____ WWII, but now I am.

2. I met Hana for _____ first time near _____ HSBC Building in _____ city of Montreal.

3. _____ Other day, my friend sailed _____ north in his boat, _____ Dolphin.

4. I have _____ little money because I lost my wallet on _____ Cavendish Street.

5. My favourite team, _____ Pink Bunnies, is in _____ 1st place.

6. I have 2 televisions. One is made by _____ Sony, and _____ other is made by _____ LG Company.

7. _____ Most interesting person I have ever met was _____ teacher at _____ SES University.

8. _____ Santa is very busy giving gifts to _____ boys and _____ girls in _____ USA.

9. _____ Canada's _____ only desert is called _____ Osoyoos Desert.

10. I am _____ only teacher at _____ SES Institute.

11. At _____ Halloween, I was teaching on _____ 3rd floor in this building.

12. I took _____ walk along _____ Lake Erie, _____ Swiss Alps, and _____ Red Sea.

13. _____ Silk Road is actually _____ highway that connects _____ Asia and _____ Europe.

14. When I was in _____ grade 5, I did _____ project about _____ space.

15. _____ Queen Elizabeth lives in _____ Buckingham Palace near_____ Thames River.

ARTICLES 11

Fill in the blanks (a, an, the or X)
Articles are always used before nouns. Common singular nouns (i.e. a car, a chair, an apple) are the most common nouns to take articles. Proper nouns (i.e. The Hudson River) sometimes take the article THE, sometimes not. Non-counting nouns and plural nouns also take articles sometimes, if they are known to the speaker (i.e. The water in my glass is hot)

The Special Gift

_____ President of _____ Netherlands had _____ secret that he couldn't tell _____ soul, not

even his _____ best friend. When he was _____ young boy, he played _____ baseball on

_____ team called _____ Cheetahs, and he discovered that he could read _____ minds of

_____ people who were close to him. Sometimes he didn't want to listen to their thoughts, but he couldn't stop it,

so he went to _____ SES Hospital near _____ Swan Lake, and he met _____ doctor who was

_____ specialist in all things about _____ brain. In _____ hospital, he waited for half _____

hour in _____ ugly chair, when finally, _____ doc-tor walked through _____ door with

_____ frown on his face. ____ Doctor looked at ____ boy, but before he spoke _____ word, _____

boy said, "I know. You don't believe me, but I can prove to you that I can read minds. _____ number 7 is your

lucky number, you were born in _____ elevator in _____ CN Tower, and you own _____ airplane,

_____ Airbus A330." _____ doctor laughed out loud, and _____ more he listened to _____

boy, _____ more he believed that he could read minds. For _____ few years, _____ doc-tor and

_____ boy met every day, and soon, _____ two started to make _____ plan to change _____

world. _____ Doctor wanted _____ boy to become _____ same kind of doctor as him, but the boy had _____ another plan. He studied at _____ University of Yale, where he finished _____ 1st in

his class in _____ Mathematics. After he graduated, he got _____ job at _____ Microsoft, where he

learned about _____ computers. He was very handsome like _____ English teacher, so he was such

_____ popular man. He decided to become _____ President of his country, _____ small country to

_____ west of Germany and to _____ east of _____ France. He was often on _____ tv, and

_____ citizens in _____ country loved him very much. Still today, nobody except _____ doctor

knows his secret, and he really hopes no-body ever does.

ARTICLES 12

Fill in the blanks (a, an, the or X)
Articles are always used before nouns. Common singular nouns (i.e. a car, a chair, an apple) are the most common nouns to take
articles. Proper nouns (i.e. The Hudson River) sometimes take the article THE, sometimes not. Non-counting nouns and plural
nouns also take articles sometimes, if they are known to the speaker (i.e. The water in my glass is hot)

---

1. _____ Toronto Zoo has _____ largest elephant in _____ North America.

2. I have studied _____ French language since _____ 3rd grade in _____ province of Quebec.

3. I am _____ Christian, and I have been to _____ St. Joseph's Oratory many times by _____ car.

4. In _____ north, birds fly _____ south in _____ winter, and only _____ few birds stay.

5. _____ Furniture in my room is made of _____ wood from _____ tree I cut down.

6. Nicola Tesla was _____ inventor of _____ plenty of machines, like _____ Earthquake Machine.

7. Tesla died in _____ 1940s with _____ little money, but is now remembered as _____ great man.

8. _____ doctor at _____ SES Clinic thought I had _____ cancer, but really I had _____ flu.

9. She grabbed him by _____ neck at _____ Villa Maria Station, so I called _____ police.

10. My mom told me to do _____ homework, or else I'd have to go to _____ jail.

11. At _____ foot of _____ mountain near my home in _____ Korea, called _____ Umyun
    Mountain, there was _____ opera house.

12. _____ Renaissance (around _____ 15th century) was _____ time when many things changed in _____ world, for _____ example, _____ sailors sailed across _____ Pacific Ocean from Europe.

13. _____ General Lee Sun Sin fought against _____ Japanese Navy during _____ Chosun Dynasty.

14. I was in _____ army in _____ 1991, but I didn't fight in _____ Iraqi War.

15. I have _____ same piano as you, but I can't play _____ piano at all.

ARTICLES 13

Fill in the blanks (a, an, the or X)
Articles are always used before nouns. Common singular nouns (i.e. a car, a chair, an apple) are the most common nouns to take articles. Proper nouns (i.e. The Hudson River) sometimes take the article THE, sometimes not. Non-counting nouns and plural nouns also take articles sometimes, if they are known to the speaker (i.e. The water in my glass is hot)

The Tada Tree

Once upon _____ time, in _____ land very different from ours, there lived _____ group of people who lived in _____ trees. They never left _____ trees they lived in, and they were _____ happiest people in _____ world. _____ Leader of _____ people was called Tada, and he was _____ extraordinarily smart man. One day, he decided to take _____ trip, _____ 1 year trip, so he decided to leave _____ tree where he lived. All of _____ people in his tree were flabbergasted, and they all said that he would catch _____ cold, or maybe get _____ cancer, or maybe he would meet _____ furri-flop, _____ most dangerous animal on their planet. _____ ground was very strange to Tada, but what was even stranger was what he saw on his trip. He slept in places called _____ hotels, like _____ Prince Hotel. He played in places like _____ Hana Park and _____ Disney Land. After 1 year, he returned to his land by _____ boat, in _____ car, and finally on _____ foot. It was _____ cold winter when he finally reached _____ tree where he was born in _____ 19th century. However, nobody was there, so he checked _____ other trees in _____ area, but they were empty as well. When he finally went up his tree, he found _____ note written by his wife, and it said, "We were so lonely without you that we all left _____ trees to find you. If you have returned, please wait for us until _____ summer time." So Tada waited, but _____ longer he waited, _____ more worried he got. _____ Summer came, and Tada was extremely excited, but nobody returned. He waited and waited, but still nobody came home. Tada never left _____ tree, and he is

still waiting for _____ most important people in his life to return home.

ARTICLES 14

1. When children go to _____ bed, they _____ first brush their teeth in _____ bathroom.

2. _____ Bush family from _____ Texas has _____ lots of _____ power in _____ White House.

3. I read _____ story in _____ Yomiuri Newspaper about _____ Yur, Japan's famous pianist.

4. In _____ Izu Park in _____ Sapporo, you can see _____ Kyu Rock.

5. _____ West Edmonton Mall is one of _____ largest malls in _____ world.

6. _____ Last summer, I went to _____ Yankee Stadium, and watched _____ New York Yankees.

7. _____ Rich in Montreal buy big houses on _____ Mont-Royal or near _____ James Bay.

8. _____ More you study, _____ happier I feel.

9. _____ Sony Company makes good machines, so I want to buy _____ PSP.

10. Last Tuesday, I fell onto _____ ground. _____ Next day, I had _____ pain in my back.

11. In _____ Amazon Forest, I saw _____ alligator, _____ owl, and _____ orangutan.

12. _____ Queen Elizabeth Hotel is near _____ port of Montreal.

13. I took _____ trip to Las Vegas, and I saw _____ Bryce Canyon and _____ Hoover Dam.

14. I got married in _____ Golden Hall with _____ beautiful girl from _____ China.

15. I watch _____ movie "Titanic" at _____ Imax Theater _____ other day.

ARTICLES 15

The Lonely Forest

At _____ Harvard University, there was _____ professor who was also _____ explorer, and his name was Mark. He wanted to go on _____ adventure, so he drove to _____ North Pole. He didn't have _____ clue where he was going, so he decided to climb _____ highest mountain in _____ north called _____ Logan Mountain. At _____ foot of _____ mountain, he bought _____ food, _____ hat, _____ map, and _____ plenty of _____ water. He started to climb, but it was very cold, so he took _____ break. When he sat on _____ ground, he heard _____ strange cracking sound, and he started to fall through _____ ground, into _____ mountain. He fell _____ hundred feet, and landed on _____ giant mushroom. Because he was so smart, he had invented _____ machine called _____ Dicto-watch, and it was able to explain anything. After checking _____ watch, Mark knew that _____ mushroom was _____ edible, so he started to eat. When he finished, he looked around, and saw _____ amazing thing: he was in _____ forest filled with _____ enormous trees, _____ humungous flowers, _____ gigantic butterflies, and _____ immense rock. Mark decided to write his name on _____ rock. Suddenly, _____ 2 eyes opened on _____ rock, and then _____ rock slowly began to speak in _____ deep voice, "Why are you writing on my chin?" Mark jumped back and nearly had _____ heart attack. Mark answered, "I didn't know you were _____ alive, so I…I…ummm." "I have been here since _____ 4th century. Long ago, I was _____ man like you. During _____ Great War, I left my home, and I found this mountain and its hidden forest. One day, I fell asleep near this _____ rock, and when I woke up, I was _____ rock. I want to leave this place and see _____ world. I need _____ person to take my place. That person is you." _____ butterfly dropped Mark into _____ mouth of _____ rock. Mark disappeared inside the rock, and a young man appeared. He stretched his legs, and left forever.

ARTICLES 16

Fill in the blanks (a, an, the or X)
Articles are always used before nouns. Common singular nouns (i.e. a car, a chair, an apple) are the most common nouns to take articles. Proper nouns (i.e. The Hudson River) sometimes take the article THE, sometimes not. Non-counting nouns and plural nouns also take articles sometimes, if they are known to the speaker (i.e. The water in my glass is hot)

1. _____ Chinese built _____ Great Wall of China, and it took _____ long time.

2. I met _____ Swiss man on _____ bus going over _____ Champlain Bridge.

3. _____ Sunlife Building was built in under 10 years, and it cost _____ million dollars.

4. Among _____ Great Lakes in Canada, _____ Lake Superior is _____ biggest.

5. I went to _____ Jeju Island, and I climbed _____ Halla Mountain in _____ hour and _____ half.

6. There is _____ hockey league in Canada called _____ NHL, and _____ winner gets _____ trophy called _____ Stanley Cup.

7. The boy was in _____ 1st place, so he was on _____ TV.

8. _____ Dominican Republic is _____ country in _____ Caribbean Sea.

9. _____ McGill University is close to _____ University of Concordia.

10. I live on _____ Benny Street, and it is _____ 5 minute drive to _____ highway.

11. I eat _____ chicken once _____ week, but I don't eat _____ eggs.

12. I have 4 cars. Two are red, and _____ others are yellow. However, I want to buy _____ BMW.

13. I saw _____ Halley's Comet flying across _____ Eastern sky _____ last night.

14. _____ Capital city of _____ Philippines is called _____ Manila.

15. I hope you enjoyed _____ time we spent answering _____ questions in this book.

Debate Topics Section

DEBATE TOPICS

- Smart students should not study during summer vacation.

- Being a star is a great life.

- It is important for people to have hobbies.

- Owning a car is good for people.

- It is better to be smart than beautiful/handsome.

- It is better to be a dog than the owner of a dog.

- Students don't need to learn PE at school.

- Students should not go to cram schools.

TOPIC 1

TOPIC 2

TOPIC 3

TOPIC 4

TOPIC 5

Making Perfect Questions

MPQ 1

For each sentence, write a question that answers it. For example, if the sentence is "I brush my teeth 3 times a day", the question could be "How often do you brush your teeth?". Many questions can be used for each sentence.

1. It will stop snowing by tonight.

   _____

2. We had better buy a map.

   _____

3. This is the oldest library in North America.

   _____

4. This building was built in 3 years.

   _____

5. The station is just 5 minutes away.

   _____

6. Because I'm tired.

   _____

7. In the park.

   _____

8. The shirt was too small, so I had to return it to the store.

   _____

9. I need 2 more cards.

   _____

10. I recommend that you watch this movie.

    _____

MPQ 2

1. It takes her about 20 minutes to make dinner.

---

2. Bread and heads.

---

3. The Canadians won the game by 5 points.

---

4. I hurt my leg while skating.

---

5. That was my favourite TV show when I was young.

---

6. I haven't been there for 3 years.

---

7. It took me 2 hours to finish ironing last night.

---

8. It is very fun to go skiing in Niseko.

---

9. That's a strange question.

---

10. Unless it rains.

MPQ 3

For each sentence, write a question that answers it.

1. I got here just before you.

2. I don't have any brothers.

3. Shanghai is a 12 hour drive from Beijing.

4. I need to go on a diet.

5. The party was really boring.

6. On foot.

7. She might have visited her friend last night.

8. I'm not sure.

9. I couldn't sleep well last night because of my test.

10. I wish I could go with you, but I can't.

MPQ 4

1. I have been studying since 9am.

2. Whenever I drink that, I feel sick, so no thanks.

3. I think you can buy one at Homac.

4. Yes, I have.

5. Maybe.

6. It took me one hour to get here.

7. That shirt really looks good on you.

8. I paid $600 for my computer.

9. The jacket on the floor next to the garbage can is mine.

10. I got an A on the test.

MPQ 5

1. I'll be meeting my friend tonight at 7pm.

   _____

2. I bought bananas.

   _____

3. I did it for my health.

   _____

4. I like the pink jacket.

   _____

5. Today is February 25.

   _____

6. Yes, I have.

   _____

7. In Canada.

   _____

8. About 10 more minutes.

   _____

9. Over 50.

   _____

10. She might have eaten pancakes.

   _____

MPQ 6

For each sentence, write a question that answers it.

1. I came here as soon as I woke up.

   _____

2. He can't eat peanut butter.

   _____

3. I would rather play tennis.

   _____

4. It will take me 2 hours to make the cake.

   _____

5. Yes, I could.

   _____

6. I wrote that while I was on the bus.

   _____

7. I wouldn't like to go because it is too late.

   _____

8. I sometimes call my mom on Sunday.

   _____

9. No, I wouldn't.

   _____

10. The last time I met my friend was 3 weeks ago.

   _____

MPQ 7

For each sentence, write a question that answers it.

1. He is a very nice guy.

   _____

2. I ate breakfast as soon as I got up today.

   _____

3. He might be sleeping right now.

   _____

4. It was rainy, so we stayed home.

   _____

5. It's round.

   _____

6. I was meeting my friend yesterday at this time.

   _____

7. I don't have any plans tomorrow.

   _____

8. Let's leave in 5 minutes.

   _____

9. I want to watch a movie tonight.

   _____

10. Spicy curry.

   _____

MPQ 8

For each sentence, write a question that answers it.

1. The movie lasted 2 hours.

_____

2. I don't have any money.

_____

3. Because it's raining.

_____

4. I have lived there for 2 years.

_____

5. I don't like it because it tastes bad.

_____

6. I want all of them.

_____

7. Medium.

_____

8. She drinks 3 glasses of water everyday.

_____

9. No, I didn't.

_____

10. Not yet.

_____

Making Perfect Sentences

MPS 1

Write a sentence using each word.

since	
for	
by the time	
at this time	
this evening	
open	
begin	
stop	
above	
reliable	
suppose	
jealous	
dream	
envy	
resemble	

MPS 2

Write a sentence using each word.

tailor	
advice	
beggar	
starve	
deny	
forget	
jog	
is like	
nearly	
burp	
insane	
active	
calf	
the wisest	
boring	

MPS 3

Write a sentence using each word.	

in the past	
at present	
graduate	
hometown	
wallet	
honey	
hop	
whine	
whistle	
not long after	
shortly before	
under	
at	
inside	
once	

MPS 4

every	
shallow	
until	
quality	
the number of	
one of	
each	
one	
none	
both	
the poor	
the rich	
wealthy	
dim	
quietly	

MPS 5

Write a sentence using each word.

plenty of	
few	
enough	
more	
several	
a great deal of	
hardly any	
no	
exit	
audience	
group	
punish	
yourself	
another	
other	

MPS 6

Write a sentence using each word.

as tall as	
every other	
other than	
on the other hand	
in other words	
one after another	
one another	
more and more	
had better	
wasn't going to	
ought to	
must have	
could be	
may not be	
should not have	

MPS 7

Write a sentence using each word.

mind	
vanish	
demon	
if possible	
why don't we	
rather be ...ing	
was helped	
must be eaten	
have been	
is made in	
known for	
disappointed in	
opposed to	
get hungry	
get worse	

MPS 8

get dizzy	
confusing	
confused	
comfortable	
fort	
stressed	
mess	
frustrating	
frustrated	
interested	
interesting	
it is a fact that	
likely	
cement	
lamb	

MPS 9

Write a sentence using each word.

slowly	
effortlessly	
amazingly	
in a talented way	
in a kind way	
worried about	
blame for	
keep on	
succeed in	
capable of	
insist on	
in addition to	
mindless	
avoid	
dream of	

MPS 10

Write a sentence using each word.	
joke	
refuse	
force to	
expert	
remind to	
remind me of	
remember	
relax	
have trouble	
have a hard time	
waste time	
it is hard for	
in order to	
went there to	
went there for	

MPS 11

Write a sentence using each word.

not old enough	
too old to	
necessary	
sarcastic	
yet	
for now	
universe	
whereas	
only if	
neither... nor	
if I study	
if it rains tonight	
if I were a king	
even though	
even if	

MPS 12

Write a sentence using each word.	

only	
until	
due to	
salad	
nevertheless	
otherwise	
or else	
therefore	
slimy	
foggy	
flimsy	
funny	
nonetheless	
fling	
smell like	

MPS 13

towards	
from	
round	
past	
underneath	
cancer	
knowledge	
annual	
pear	
real	
radish	
adore	
thunder	
muggy	
break into	

Write a sentence using each word.

MPS 14

pleased	
watch	
see	
look at	
hurt	
just like	
love the way	
pain	
ache	
somewhat	
tremendously	
totally	
calmly	
thunder	
lightning	

MPS 15

Write a sentence using each word.

alone	
along	
bored	
board	
barely	
rarely	
hardly ever	
all summer	
briefly	
brainless	
useless	
overnight	
regularly	
one of these days	
generally	

MPS 16

Write a sentence using each word.

invisible	
dislike	
unhappily	
impossible	
except	
turn	
fry	
dress	
quarrel	
lung	
a head of	
loads of	
pool	
creep	
end	

Short Stories

SHORT STORY 1

THE NEW HOLIDAY

SHORT STORY 2

SHORT STORY 3

THE SONG THAT CHANGED THE WORLD

SHORT STORY 4

TADA TREE

SHORT STORY 5

DOCTOR STRANGE

Essays

ESSAY 1

HOW CAN YOU IMPROVE YOUR LIFE?

ESSAY 2

ESSAY 3

ESSAY 4

ESSAY 5

APPENDIX

LIST OF PREPOSITIONS

Prepositions are words that tells us about where something is, or when something happens. They are always used to talk about nouns, like **on** TV, **in** my hand, or **above** my head. Here is a list of common prepositions:

aboard	about	above	across	after	against
ahead of	all over	along	among	apart	around
as	at	away	away from	back	before
behind	below	beneath	between	beyond	by
close by	close to	despite	down	during	except
for	forward	from	in	in between	in front of
inside	into	like	near	next to	of
off	on	on top of	opposite	outside	onto
over	out	out of	round	past	since
through	to	toward	towards	under	until
upon	up	with	within	without	

OSASCNM – THE ORDER OF ADJECTIVES

In English, you must use adjectives in the certain order in a sentence. You must not mix up the order of the adjectives. It is one of English grammar rules.

If you can remember OSASCNM, then you will know the order of adjectives.

<u>O</u> = Opinion, <u>S</u> = Size, <u>A</u> = Age, <u>S</u> = Shape, <u>C</u> = Colour, <u>N</u> = Nationality, <u>M</u> = Material

⊙ I have a <u>nice</u>, <u>big</u>, <u>old</u>, <u>square</u>, <u>brown</u>, <u>Canadian</u>, <u>wooden</u> chair.
     O   S   A   S   C   N   M

× I have a <u>big</u>, <u>square</u>, <u>Canadian</u>, <u>old</u>, <u>brown</u>, <u>nice</u> <u>wooden</u> chair.
     S   S   N   A   C   O   M

List of irregular verbs

Present	Past	P. Perfect	Present	Past	P. Perfect	Present	Past	P. Perfect
awake	awoke	awoken	come	came	come	freeze	froze	frozen
be	was/ were	been	cost	cost	cost	get	got	gotten
			creep	crept	crept	give	gave	given
bear	bore	born	cut	cut	cut	go	went	gone
beat	beat	beat	deal	dealt	dealt	grind	ground	ground
become	became	become	dig	dug	dug	grow	grew	grown
begin	began	begun	dive	dived dove	dived	hang	hung	hung
bend	bent	bent				hear	heard	heard
beset	beset	beset	do	did	done	hide	hid	hidden
bet	bet	bet	draw	drew	drawn	hit	hit	hit
bid	bid bade	bid bidden	dream	dreamt dreamed	dreamt dreamed	hold	held	held
						hurt	hurt	hurt
bind	bound	bound	drive	drove	driven	keep	kept	kept
bite	bit	bitten	drink	drank	drunk	kneel	knelt	knelt
bleed	bled	bled	eat	ate	eaten	knit	knit	knit
blow	blew	blown	fall	fell	fallen	know	knew	know
break	broke	broken	feed	fed	fed	lay	laid	laid
breed	bred	bred	feel	felt	felt	lead	led	led
bring	brought	brought	fight	fought	fought	leap	leapt leaped	leapt leaped
broadcast	broadcast	broadcast	find	found	found			
build	built	built	fit	fit	fit	learn	learnt learned	learned learnt
burn	burned burnt	burned burnt	flee	fled	fled			
			fling	flung	flung	leave	left	left
burst	burst	burst	fly	flew	flown	lend	lent	lent
buy	bought	bought	forbid	forbade	forbidden	lie	lay	lain
cast	cast	cast	forget	forgot	forgotten	light	lighted lit	lighted lit
catch	caught	caught	forego	forewent	foregone			
choose	chose	chosen	forgive	forgave	forgiven	lose	lost	lost
cling	clung	clung	forsake	forsook	forsaken	make	made	made

mean	meant	meant	sew	sewed sewn	sewed sewn	spit	spit/spat	spit
meet	met	met				split	split	split
misspell	misspelled misspelt	misspelled misspelt	shear	shore	shorn	spread	spread	spread
mistake	mistook	mistaken	shave	shaved	shaved shaven	spring	sprang sprung	sprung
mow	mowed	mowed mown	shed	shed	shed	stand	stood	stood
			shine	shone	shone	steal	stole	stolen
overcome	overcame	overcome	shoot	shot	shot	stick	stuck	stuck
overdo	overdid	overdone	shoe	shoed	shod shoed	sting	stung	stung
overtake	overtook	overtaken				stink	stank	stunk
overthrow	overthrew	overthrown	shrink	shrank	shrunk	stride	strode	stridden
pay	paid	paid	show	showed	showed shown	string	strung	strung
plead	pled	pled				strive	strove	striven
prove	proved	proved proven	shut	shut	shut	swear	swore	sworn
			sing	sang	sung	sweep	swept	swept
put	put	put	sink	sank	sunk	swell	swelled	swelled swollen
read	read	read	sit	sat	sat			
rid	rid	rid	sleep	slept	slept	swim	swam	swum
ride	rode	ridden	slay	slew	slain	swing	swung	swung
ring	rang	rung	slide	slid	slid	take	took	taken
rise	rose	risen	sling	slung	slung	teach	taught	taught
run	ran	run	slit	slit	slit	tear	tore	torn
saw	sawed	sawed sawn	sow	sowed	sowed sown	tell	told	told
						think	thought	thought
say	said	said	spill	spilt/spilled	spilt	swim	swam	swum
see	saw	seen				throw	threw	thrown
seek	sought	sought	speak	spoke	spoken	thrive thrived	throve	thrived
sell	sold	sold						
send	sent	sent	speed	sped	sped	thrust	thrust	thrust
set	set	set	spend	spent	spent	tread	trod	trodden
shake	shook	shaken	spin	spun	spun	understand	understood	understood
upset	upset	upset	wind	wound	wound	write	wrote	written
wake	woke	woken	weave	weaved wove	weaved woven	withhold	withheld	withheld
wear	wore	worn				withstand	withstood	withstood
wed	wed	wed	win	won	won			
weep	wept	wept	wring	wrung	wrung			

Homework